For

mrs. Smith

D1510111

For Louise Bachelder,
master teacher and friend

Copyright © 1994
Peter Pauper Press, Inc.
202 Mamaroneck Avenue
White Plains, NY 10601
All rights reserved
ISBN 0-88088-786-9
Printed in China
12 11 10 9 8 7

For My Teacher

*T*o teach is to touch lives forever.

ANONYMOUS

I might have dissected a frog five hundred times, but the 501st time I always see something I didn't before— and it's the same thing with teaching students. You always see something new.

ANNE FRYE

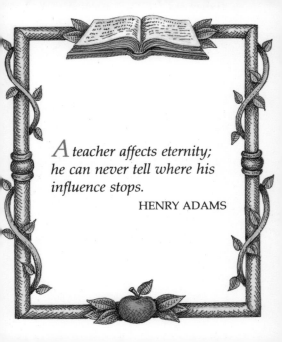

A teacher affects eternity;
he can never tell where his
influence stops.

HENRY ADAMS

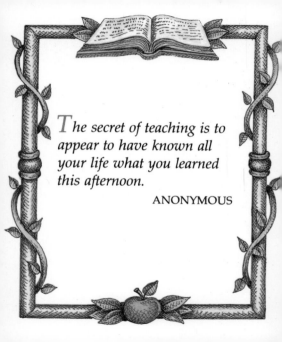

The secret of teaching is to appear to have known all your life what you learned this afternoon.

ANONYMOUS

If you promise not to believe everything your child says happens at this school, I'll promise not to believe everything he says happens at home.

*Note to students' parents
from an English schoolmaster*

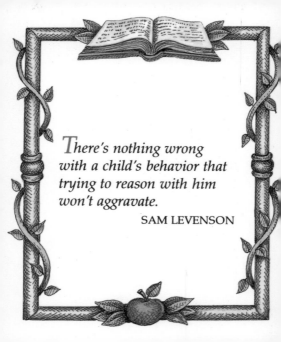

There's nothing wrong
with a child's behavior that
trying to reason with him
won't aggravate.

SAM LEVENSON

Life is my college. May I graduate well and earn some honors.

LOUISA MAY ALCOTT

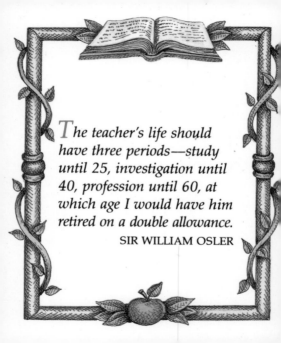

The teacher's life should have three periods—study until 25, investigation until 40, profession until 60, at which age I would have him retired on a double allowance.

SIR WILLIAM OSLER

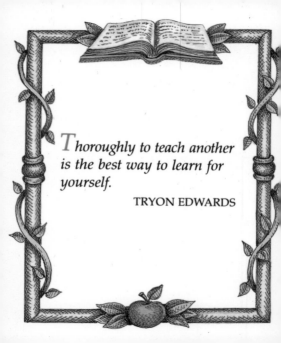

Thoroughly to teach another is the best way to learn for yourself.

TRYON EDWARDS

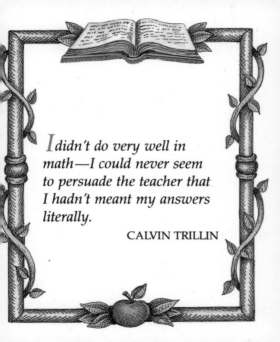

I didn't do very well in math—I could never seem to persuade the teacher that I hadn't meant my answers literally.

CALVIN TRILLIN

No bubble is so iridescent or floats longer than that blown by the successful teacher.

SIR WILLIAM OSLER

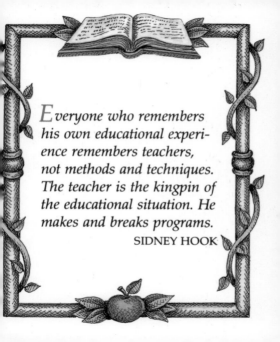

*E*veryone who remembers his own educational experience remembers teachers, not methods and techniques. The teacher is the kingpin of the educational situation. He makes and breaks programs.

SIDNEY HOOK

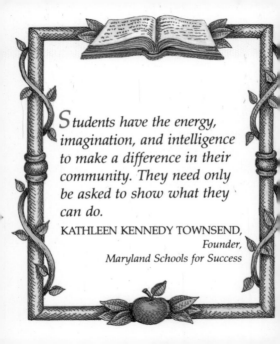

*S*tudents have the energy, imagination, and intelligence to make a difference in their community. They need only be asked to show what they can do.

KATHLEEN KENNEDY TOWNSEND,
Founder,
Maryland Schools for Success

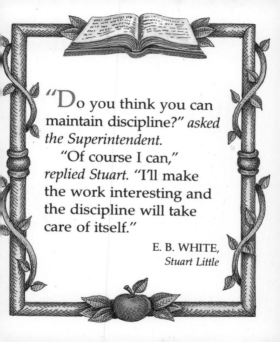

"Do you think you can maintain discipline?" *asked the Superintendent.*

"Of course I can," *replied Stuart.* "I'll make the work interesting and the discipline will take care of itself."

E. B. WHITE,
Stuart Little

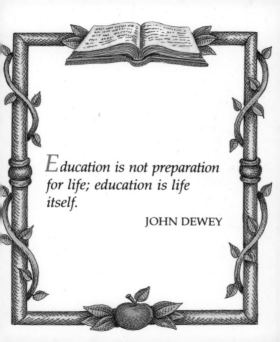

*E*ducation is not preparation for life; education is life itself.

JOHN DEWEY

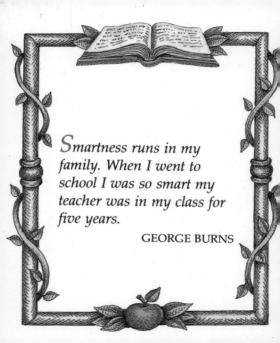

Smartness runs in my family. When I went to school I was so smart my teacher was in my class for five years.

GEORGE BURNS

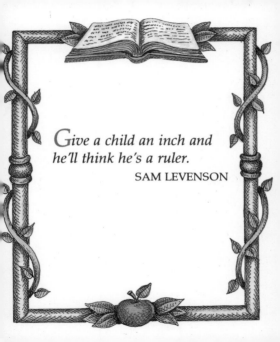

Give a child an inch and he'll think he's a ruler.

SAM LEVENSON

Teach the young people how to think, not what to think.

SIDNEY SUGARMAN

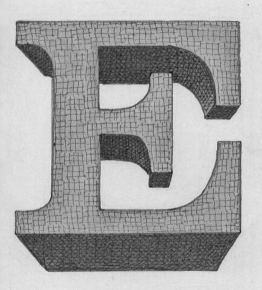

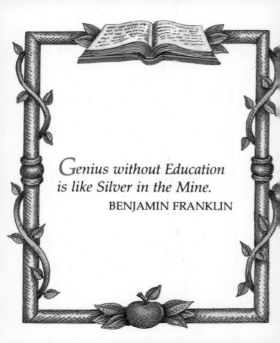

*Genius without Education
is like Silver in the Mine.*

BENJAMIN FRANKLIN

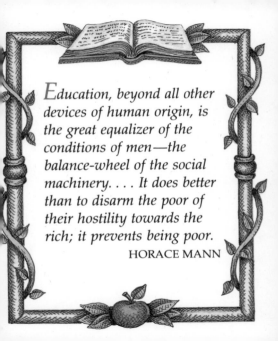

Education, beyond all other devices of human origin, is the great equalizer of the conditions of men—the balance-wheel of the social machinery. . . . It does better than to disarm the poor of their hostility towards the rich; it prevents being poor.

HORACE MANN

*C*hildren who are treated
as if they are uneducable
almost invariably become
uneducable.

KENNETH B. CLARK

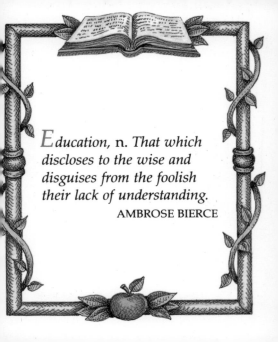

*E*ducation, n. *That which discloses to the wise and disguises from the foolish their lack of understanding.*

AMBROSE BIERCE

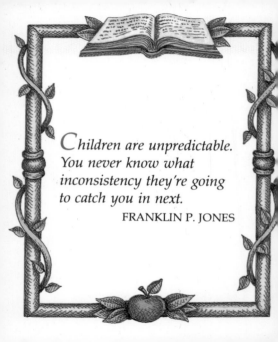

*C*hildren are unpredictable.
You never know what
inconsistency they're going
to catch you in next.

FRANKLIN P. JONES

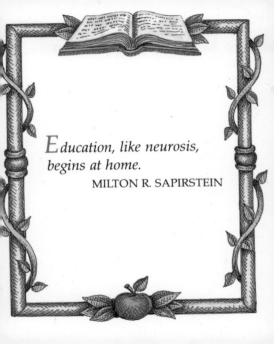

*E*ducation, like neurosis,
begins at home.

MILTON R. SAPIRSTEIN

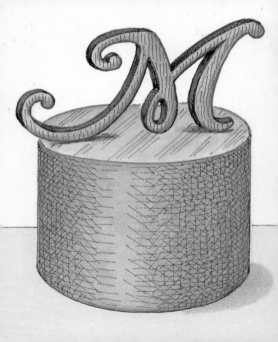

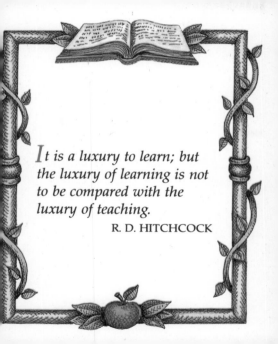

*I*t is a luxury to learn; but the luxury of learning is not to be compared with the luxury of teaching.

R. D. HITCHCOCK

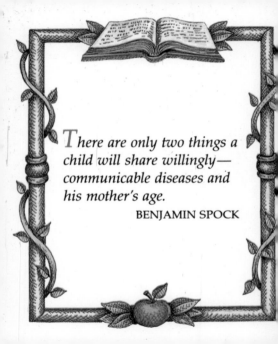

There are only two things a
child will share willingly—
communicable diseases and
his mother's age.

BENJAMIN SPOCK

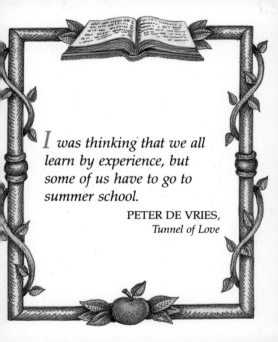

I was thinking that we all learn by experience, but some of us have to go to summer school.

PETER DE VRIES,
Tunnel of Love

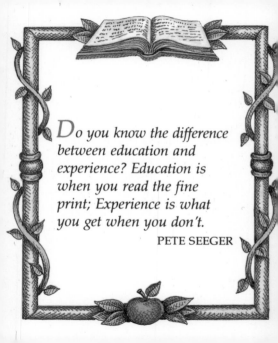

Do you know the difference between education and experience? Education is when you read the fine print; Experience is what you get when you don't.

PETE SEEGER

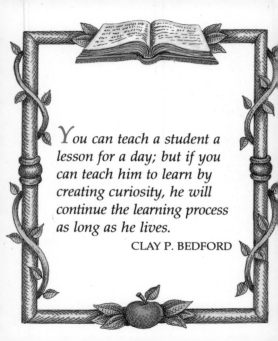

You can teach a student a lesson for a day; but if you can teach him to learn by creating curiosity, he will continue the learning process as long as he lives.

CLAY P. BEDFORD

Imagination is a child's place.

ANONYMOUS

The sweet and powerful knowledge we gain . . . should not close us back upon our narrow selves, but should make us truly "citizens of the world."

NANNERL O. KEOHANE,
Past President of
Wellesley College and
President of Duke University

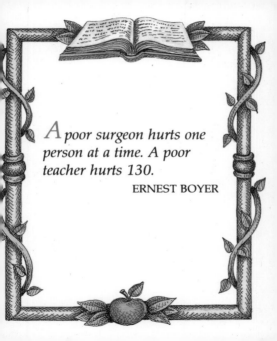

A poor surgeon hurts one person at a time. A poor teacher hurts 130.

ERNEST BOYER

My goal each September is to build a working relationship based on trust. I enter into a partnership with each student, with clearly defined, realistic goals. We define my job as their teacher and their

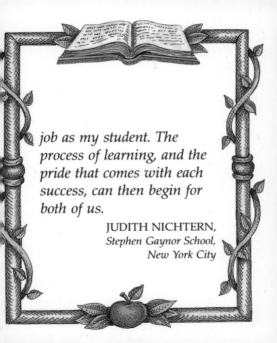

job as my student. The process of learning, and the pride that comes with each success, can then begin for both of us.

JUDITH NICHTERN,
*Stephen Gaynor School,
New York City*

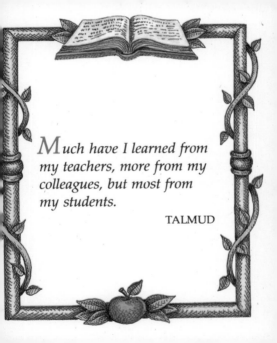

*M*uch have I learned from my teachers, more from my colleagues, but most from my students.

TALMUD

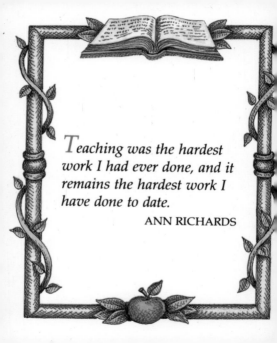

*T*eaching was the hardest work I had ever done, and it remains the hardest work I have done to date.

ANN RICHARDS

*T*he pupil who is never required to do what he cannot do, never does what he can do.

JOHN STUART MILL

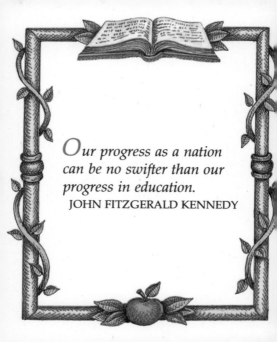

*O*ur progress as a nation can be no swifter than our progress in education.
JOHN FITZGERALD KENNEDY

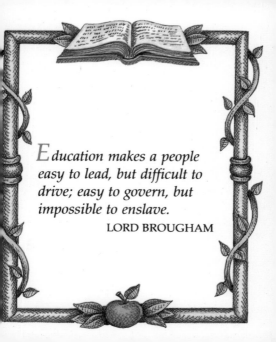

*E*ducation makes a people easy to lead, but difficult to drive; easy to govern, but impossible to enslave.

LORD BROUGHAM

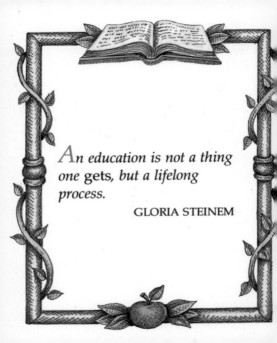

*A*n education is not a thing one gets, but a lifelong process.

GLORIA STEINEM

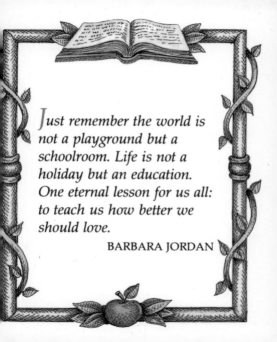

*J*ust remember the world is not a playground but a schoolroom. Life is not a holiday but an education. One eternal lesson for us all: to teach us how better we should love.

BARBARA JORDAN

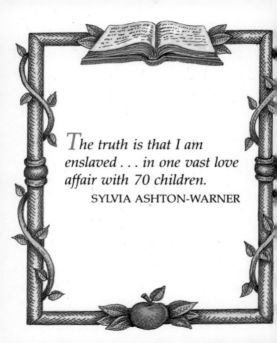

The truth is that I am enslaved . . . in one vast love affair with 70 children.

SYLVIA ASHTON-WARNER

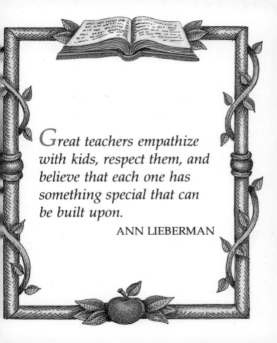

Great teachers empathize with kids, respect them, and believe that each one has something special that can be built upon.

ANN LIEBERMAN

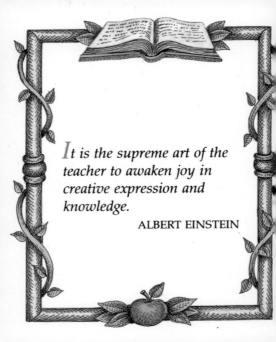

It is the supreme art of the teacher to awaken joy in creative expression and knowledge.

ALBERT EINSTEIN

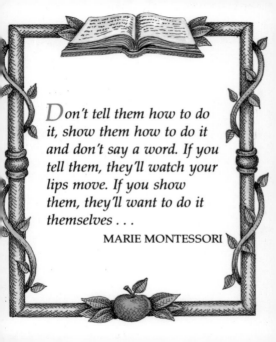

Don't tell them how to do it, show them how to do it and don't say a word. If you tell them, they'll watch your lips move. If you show them, they'll want to do it themselves . . .

MARIE MONTESSORI

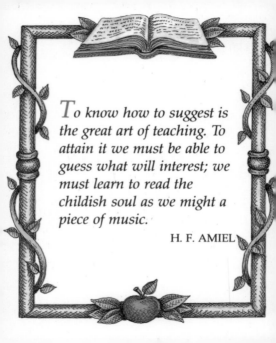

*T*o know how to suggest is the great art of teaching. To attain it we must be able to guess what will interest; we must learn to read the childish soul as we might a piece of music.

H. F. AMIEL

Question asked by Dimitri (nine years old), of his teacher (47 years old): "Ms. Stevens, are you a virgin?"

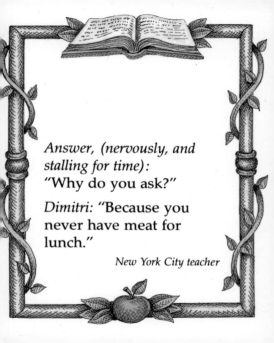

Answer, (nervously, and stalling for time):
"Why do you ask?"

Dimitri: "Because you never have meat for lunch."

New York City teacher

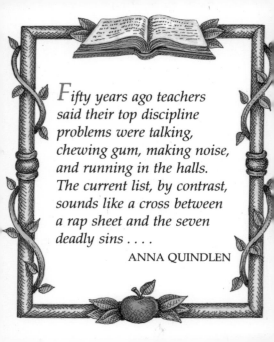

*F*ifty years ago teachers said their top discipline problems were talking, chewing gum, making noise, and running in the halls. The current list, by contrast, sounds like a cross between a rap sheet and the seven deadly sins . . . .

ANNA QUINDLEN

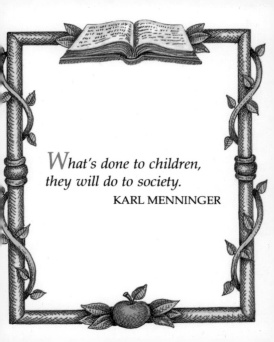

What's done to children,
they will do to society.

KARL MENNINGER

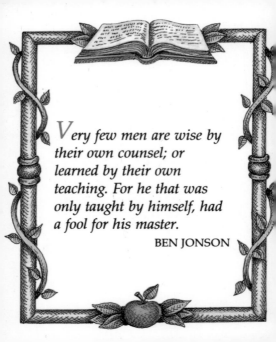

*V*ery few men are wise by their own counsel; or learned by their own teaching. For he that was only taught by himself, had a fool for his master.

BEN JONSON

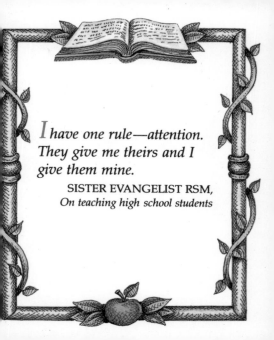

I have one rule—attention.
They give me theirs and I
give them mine.

SISTER EVANGELIST RSM,
On teaching high school students

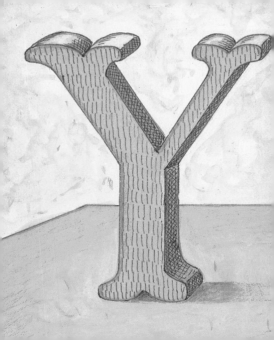

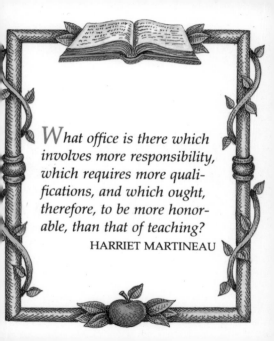

What office is there which involves more responsibility, which requires more quali-fications, and which ought, therefore, to be more honor-able, than that of teaching?

HARRIET MARTINEAU

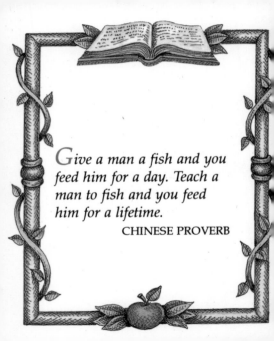

*G*ive a man a fish and you feed him for a day. Teach a man to fish and you feed him for a lifetime.

CHINESE PROVERB

Experience is a hard teacher because she gives the test first, the lesson after.

VERNON LAW

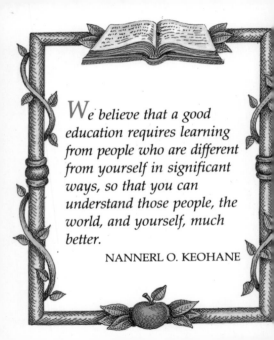

We believe that a good education requires learning from people who are different from yourself in significant ways, so that you can understand those people, the world, and yourself, much better.

NANNERL O. KEOHANE

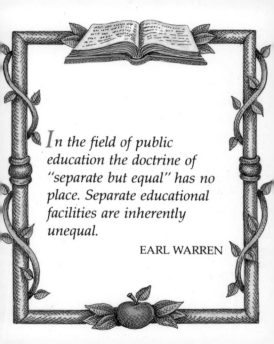

In the field of public education the doctrine of "separate but equal" has no place. Separate educational facilities are inherently unequal.

EARL WARREN

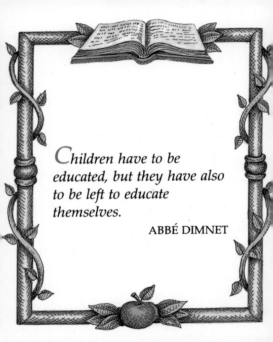

*C*hildren have to be educated, but they have also to be left to educate themselves.

ABBÉ DIMNET

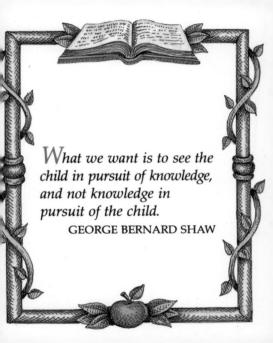

*W*hat we want is to see the child in pursuit of knowledge, and not knowledge in pursuit of the child.

GEORGE BERNARD SHAW

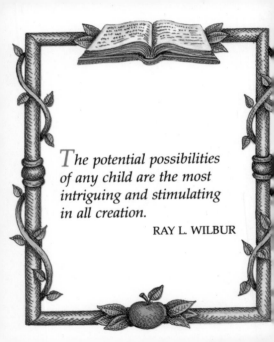

The potential possibilities
of any child are the most
intriguing and stimulating
in all creation.

RAY L. WILBUR

*E*ducation: Hanging around until you've caught on.

ROBERT FROST

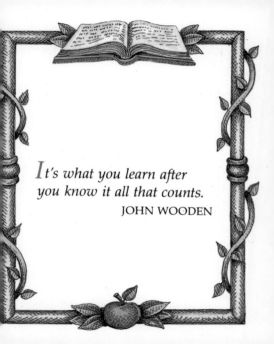

*It's what you learn after
you know it all that counts.*

JOHN WOODEN

*G*oodbye tension, hello pension!

FAY MICHAUD,
Retiring teacher

My heart is singing for joy this morning. A miracle has happened! The light of understanding has shone upon my little pupil's mind, and behold, all things are changed!

ANNIE SULLIVAN

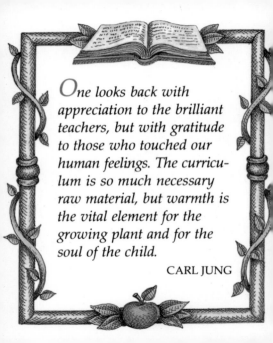

*O*ne looks back with appreciation to the brilliant teachers, but with gratitude to those who touched our human feelings. The curriculum is so much necessary raw material, but warmth is the vital element for the growing plant and for the soul of the child.

CARL JUNG

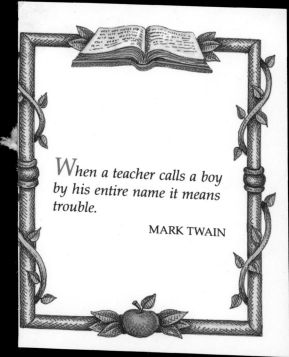

When a teacher calls a boy by his entire name it means trouble.

MARK TWAIN

I touch the future. I teach.

CHRISTA McAULIFFE